Dear Parent:

Congratulations! Your child is taking the first steps on an exciting journey. The destination? Independent reading!

STEP INTO READING® will help your child get there. The program offers five steps to reading success. Each step includes fun stories and colorful art. There are also Step into Reading Sticker Books, Step into Reading Math Readers, Step into Reading Write-In Readers, Step into Reading Phonics Readers, and Step into Reading Phonics First Steps! Boxed Sets—a complete literacy program with something for every child.

Learning to Read, Step by Step!

Ready to Read   Preschool–Kindergarten
• big type and easy words • rhyme and rhythm • picture clues
For children who know the alphabet and are eager to begin reading.

Reading with Help   Preschool–Grade 1
• basic vocabulary • short sentences • simple stories
For children who recognize familiar words and sound out new words with help.

Reading on Your Own   Grades 1–3
• engaging characters • easy-to-follow plots • popular topics
For children who are ready to read on their own.

Reading Paragraphs   Grades 2–3
• challenging vocabulary • short paragraphs • exciting stories
For newly independent readers who read simple sentences with confidence.

Ready for Chapters   Grades 2–4
• chapters • longer paragraphs • full-color art
For children who want to take the plunge into chapter books but still like colorful pictures.

STEP INTO READING® is designed to give every child a successful reading experience. The grade levels are only guides. Children can progress through the steps at their own speed, developing confidence in their reading, no matter what their grade.

Remember, a lifetime love of reading starts with a single step!

For my parents
—S.K.

For Jean
—T.L.P.

Photo credits: The Royal Geographical Society, pp. 3, 23, 25, 38, 45; H. Armstrong Roberts, Inc., © V. Clevenger, p. 12

www.stepintoreading.com

Educators and librarians, for a variety of teaching tools, visit us at www.randomhouse.com/teachers

Library of Congress Cataloging-in-Publication Data
Kramer, Sydelle.
To the top! : climbing the world's highest mountain / by S. A. Kramer ; illustrated by Thomas La Padula.   p.   cm. — (Step into reading. A step 5 book)
SUMMARY: Describes how Edmund Hillary and Tenzing Norgay became the first human beings to reach the top of the world by climbing Mount Everest.
ISBN 0-679-83885-6 (trade) — ISBN 0-679-93885-0 (lib. bdg.)
1. Mountaineering—Everest, Mount (China and Nepal)—History—Juvenile literature.
2. Hillary, Edmund, Sir—Juvenile literature.   3. Tenzing Norkey, 1914– —Juvenile literature.
4. Mountaineers—Biography—Juvenile literature.
5. Everest, Mount (China and Nepal)—Juvenile literature. [1. Mountaineering.
2. Everest, Mount (China and Nepal).   3. Hillary, Edmund, Sir.   4. Tenzing Norkey, 1914– .
5. Mountaineers.]
I. La Padula, Tom, ill.   II. Title.   III. Step into reading. Step 5 book.
GV199.44.E85   R73   2003   796.52'2'092—dc21   2002012259

Printed in the United States of America   29

TO THE TOP!

Climbing the World's
Highest Mountain

by S. A. Kramer

illustrated by Thomas La Padula

Random House New York

The Men and the Mountain

Two men stand at the bottom of a giant mountain. Snow is falling, and an angry wind roars all around. No matter where they look, they see only ice and rock. This is a place where nothing grows and no one lives.

But the men don't seem to notice what a lonely spot it is. They pay no attention to the bitter cold or the storm. Their eyes are fixed on the mountain, so tall they can't even see the top.

The mountain is Everest. It is the highest in the world. At 29,028 feet, it's close to five and a half miles tall—higher even than the clouds.

And Mount Everest isn't just tall—it's one of the coldest places on earth. No matter what the time of year, snow and ice never melt there. It is part of a great mountain range in Asia called the Himalayas. Himalaya means "the home of snow."

The two men at Everest are mountain climbers. Their names are Edmund Hillary and Tenzing Norgay. It is 1953, and they want to be the first to reach the very top of Everest—the summit.

No one has ever climbed Mount Everest all the way. Ten times before, men have tried and failed. Nineteen climbers have already died. Two of them vanished near the summit and were never seen again.

Tenzing and Hillary are part of a special group called an expedition that will try to

reach the top. If they make it, they will be heroes throughout the world. Millions of people everywhere are waiting for news of their attempt. Will Everest finally be conquered?

Many people believe that it's impossible to reach the summit. Parts of the mountain are so steep and dangerous that one false step can mean death. A climber can tumble thousands of feet down a slope. Or plunge close to two miles through the air.

Everest is so cold, the temperature can drop to forty degrees below zero even in summer. Without special clothes, a person would freeze to death in minutes.

The wind is very strong—as strong as a hurricane's. It can hammer in at over a hundred miles per hour. Climbers can be blown right off their feet.

Terrible avalanches—sliding ice, rock, and snow—sweep down Everest's slopes several times each day. Climbers get buried before they know what hit them. In 1922 seven people were killed in a single avalanche.

But the main reason no one has climbed the mountain is its incredible height. The higher you go, the less oxygen there is in the air. At Everest's summit, there's only a third of what's on the ground. Without enough oxygen, a climber's body breaks down. Anyone who stays that high too long will die.

Hillary and Tenzing know how dangerous Everest is. But both are convinced they can make it to the summit. There's no place on earth, they feel, that humans cannot reach. They see Everest as a challenge people cannot turn away from. It must be climbed "because it is there."

Now the moment has come. The mountaintop hides somewhere in the clouds. To reach it, Hillary and Tenzing are about to risk everything.

The Beginning

Just a few months earlier, Hillary and Tenzing were strangers. Yet for many years they shared a dream—to be first on Everest's summit.

Hillary is a beekeeper from faraway New Zealand. When he was young, no one expected him to amount to much. He was a small, shy boy who did poorly in school. His father sometimes beat him.

But he grew up tall and strong. He made climbing his hobby. He didn't see snow

until he was sixteen, and he didn't make it up his first peak until he was twenty.

Tenzing has known mountains all his life. He was born into a mountain people called the Sherpas who live in the country of Nepal. Since Everest lies on Nepal's border, he grew up in its shadow.

Tenzing works as a mountain guide, and people call him "Tiger of the Snows." Over the years, he has tried to climb

Everest several times. His family worries that he'll keep trying until he makes it—or until he dies.

One day, Tenzing and Hillary hear about a new expedition organized by the British. Fourteen of the world's finest climbers will be asked to join. The group will work together as a team. But only the best climbers will head for the summit.

There won't be enough time or supplies for everyone to try.

Hillary and Tenzing are both invited. The expedition gathers in Katmandu, Nepal's capital.

Before they head for the mountain, the group collects supplies. The climbers will

be away for three months, so they must take 22,000 pounds of equipment. The expedition will fail if they run out of anything important. Once they leave, there will be no way to get more supplies.

Hillary and Tenzing check the equipment. Everything is there, from their favor-

ite foods to the warmest parkas. What's most important, though, are the tanks they'll strap on their backs.

These tanks contain oxygen to help them breathe at great heights. Even if climbers practice in thin air to get their bodies used to it, very few can climb high mountains without extra oxygen. An area called the "death zone" begins at 26,000 feet. No one can stay there long and survive.

But oxygen tanks are heavy. Carrying them makes the climb that much harder. The expedition has the lightest tanks possible. Tenzing and Hillary just hope they'll be light enough.

The expedition sets out for Everest on March 10, 1953. Four hundred and fifty Sherpas have been hired to haul supplies as far up the mountain as they can. Many lug close to sixty pounds.

To reach Everest, the expedition must walk one hundred and ninety miles. The only path is so narrow they have to march one by one. It will take them more than a month just to get to the mountain!

The path begins in a jungle. It's sweltering. Soon everyone is dripping with sweat. It's hard to believe they'll soon be wearing parkas and snow boots.

The jungle is beautiful, but Tenzing and Hillary are on guard. Tigers, crocodiles, and deadly snakes prowl nearby. Leeches,

a kind of worm, suck their blood as they wade through water. They cross rivers on rope bridges that sway madly in the wind.

Always the path takes them higher. It gets colder as it heads up. Frosty peaks stand in the distance. One of them is Everest.

Then, at last, they arrive. Everest towers above them, jagged and icy. Even at

a distance it glistens in the light. It is easy to understand why the Sherpas call it Chomolungma, "Goddess Mother of the World." It looks as though it might have once ruled the earth. The queen of all mountains, it is the most terrifying yet the grandest.

As the wind whips around them, Tenzing and Hillary stare in silence.

The Climb

The expedition gets busy setting up the first, or base, camp. They will make eight more camps on Everest, each one higher than the last. Inside the tents are food, equipment, and warmth—everything the men will need to keep climbing.

Base camp is near a mysterious area of the Himalayas. Many Sherpas believe that a strange beast sometimes wanders there. Just two years ago, weird four-toed footprints were photographed in the ice. The footprints weren't human and belonged to no known animal.

No one is sure if this beast really exists. But the Sherpas have a name for it: the yeti, or "the man-thing of the snows." Others call it the Abominable Snowman.

It is said that the yeti walks on all fours but runs like a person. It has reddish brown hair and a head that comes to a point.

Instead of speaking, it makes a sound like a crazy laugh—"Kak-kak-kak-kai-ee! Kak-kak-kak-kai-ee!"

Tenzing and Hillary would like to solve the mystery. But there's no trace of the yeti around the camp. And there's no time to search for it. The climb must begin.

Tenzing and Hillary are among the first to head out. From this point on, there's no path—they must make their own.

Ahead lies a great ice field called a glacier. It's as steep as a slide but not nearly as smooth. Running all through it are cracks called crevasses. Some of them are a hundred feet deep. One wrong move—and someone can disappear forever.

To make matters worse, towers of ice and snow stand here and there. They can suddenly topple and crush a climber.

Hillary and Tenzing climb very carefully. They use a special tool called an ice ax to chop steps in the ice. So that they don't slip and slide, they strap spikes called crampons to their boots.

When they come to wide crevasses, they fling bridges made of ladders across them. They mark their path up the glacier with colored flags and fixed ropes to use as handrails. That way, climbers can follow and feel safer.

The two men climb right up the glacier's middle, along the part called the icefall. It's not safe on the glacier's sides—that's where the avalanches hit. The ice groans as they inch forward. Sometimes they can feel it moving underneath their feet.

It seems to take forever to get anywhere —four days to go a third of a mile. The climbers move in groups, attached to each other by rope. Then if one of them falls, the others can try to hold him. They can stomp their crampons into the ice and whack their axes in, too.

But this way of climbing can sometimes cost lives instead of saving them. A single climber can topple over and drag all his companions with him.

The constantly changing weather adds to the danger. There are sudden snowstorms on the glacier every afternoon. It might be fourteen below zero at night and seventy above the next morning.

Even the sun can be a menace. Sometimes it shines so brightly on the ice that a climber gets badly sunburned. Its glare on the snow can hurt a climber's eyes.

When that happens, the person becomes snowblind. The blindness is temporary, but it can last for days. Everyone wears special goggles to protect their eyes.

One day Tenzing and Hillary are out alone on the glacier. The wind is fierce, and it's bitter cold.

Hillary walks in front, attached to Tenzing by a rope. He moves slowly, step by step. Suddenly, there's nothing under his feet! Down he plunges into a hidden

crevasse. He slides down an ice wall and slams onto a shelf.

Tenzing rushes into action. He swings his ax into the ice. Then he twirls the rope around the handle and twists it around his waist. He can hear Hillary shouting out for help. Slowly but surely, he pulls Hillary up.

It is a close call. But Tenzing has saved Hillary's life.

Now the expedition comes to a great valley of snow and ice. It sweeps silently down the mountain like an enormous waterslide. At the top are huge steps, as though a giant had built a staircase.

The weather gets worse and worse—there is snow and wind and hail. The terrible cold dries out their throats and makes them continually thirsty.

They reach a flat place that looks as strange as the moon. Stones covered with blue ice are scattered all over. They are more than four and a half miles high, yet the summit still seems far away. It's always hidden by blizzards, or clouds, or ghostly mists.

Two other men in the expedition are chosen to head for the top. Hours later they return exhausted and grim. They couldn't make it.

Tenzing and Hillary will try next. Alone, they climb higher and camp for the night. If Everest is to be conquered, it's up to them.

To the Top

May 29, 1953. It is four in the morning 27,900 feet up. Hillary and Tenzing are huddled in their tent. No one has ever spent a night so high before.

The sun begins to rise. All around, the ice glows with its light. The wind quiets down. The weather will be clear.

The two men eat breakfast quickly. They stuff down sardines, crackers, lemon juice, sugar, and tea.

Hillary's boots have frozen, so he puts them on their tiny stove to thaw. The smell of hot leather and rubber fills the tent. It is so awful, the two can't wait to leave.

At 6:30, they're ready. They come out of the tent looking more like astronauts than mountain climbers. Since the temperature is seventeen degrees below zero, they wear eight layers of their warmest clothing. Three pairs of gloves lie snug around their hands. Special boots protect their feet from freezing. Each man carries forty pounds of equipment.

The snow is soft and slippery. For every five steps they take, they slide back three. This kind of snow means an avalanche is possible. Hillary asks Tenzing, "Shall we go on?" Tenzing replies, "Just as you wish." No matter what the danger, neither wants to turn back now.

Ahead is a ridge, where two sides of the mountain meet. It's as steep as a staircase and as narrow as a diving board. They know each step could be their last.

With his ice ax, Hillary cuts steps for both of them. But Tenzing falls behind. Something is wrong! Ice has filled his oxygen line—he can hardly breathe!

Hillary grabs the line. There's no time to lose. He manages to unblock it. Tenzing gulps down the oxygen. Another close call. This time Hillary has saved Tenzing.

They climb over ground no other human has ever seen. Suddenly, a black wall of smooth rock blocks their path. It's forty feet high, and there's no way around it. Has the mountain finally defeated them? How will they ever climb over the wall?

Then Hillary has an idea! There's a long crack in the wall just wide enough to squeeze into. Both he and Tenzing can shinny up backward.

Hillary goes first, attached to Tenzing by rope. One side of the crack is ice—if it breaks off, Hillary will be left dangling. If Tenzing can't hold him, they both might drop off Everest's side.

It takes Hillary a half hour to jam himself in and shinny up the crack. He's never been so exhausted in his life.

But finally he's safe. He collapses onto the snow. He's so out of breath, he says he's "gasping like a fish."

After Tenzing gets up the crack, they head even higher. Each step they take feels like a mile. They reach a narrow ridge that's very dangerous. There's a drop of eight thousand feet on the left. The right is even worse. It's ten thousand feet down, almost two miles!

Anxiously, they edge their way along. How far can the summit be? They feel as if they've been climbing forever. Ahead there's a bump of snow. Then the mountain slopes down.

The bump is the summit! They struggle toward it. Suddenly, they hesitate. Will it slide down the mountainside like an avalanche? Or is it sturdy enough to stand on?

They're not going to stop now. They step onto the summit. It holds firm!

They've made it—first to the top of the world!

Tenzing beams at Hillary, and then the two shake hands. Tenzing is so happy, he gives Hillary a hug. Then he says in the Sherpa language, "Thuji chey, Chomolungma." I am grateful, Goddess Mother of the World.

It's 11:30 in the morning. They throw off their oxygen tanks. Hillary takes out a camera he's kept warm under his clothes. They need photographs to prove they've actually reached the summit. The first one is of Tenzing waving four flags from his ice ax: the United Nations, Nepal, India, and Great Britain.

The two men look down and watch the floating clouds. Everest casts a purple shadow for miles, while the sun makes the rivers shine silver. "Nothing above us, a world below," Hillary says to himself.

They check their oxygen and eat a snack—chocolate mint cake and lemonade! Then Tenzing digs a hole to bury gifts to the gods the Sherpas believe live on Everest. His gifts are lollipops, chocolate, biscuits, a blue pencil his daughter gave him, and a cat made of black cloth.

Hillary also digs a small hole. He buries a cross that the head of the expedition asked him to leave behind.

After fifteen minutes, it's time to go. If they stay longer, their oxygen might run out. The two men head down Mount Everest in triumph. They have stood on top of the world!

Afterward

Tenzing and Hillary are heroes. In a way, they stand for all human beings. They've proved people can reach the highest point on the planet. Their feat is celebrated all over the world.

In Great Britain, loudspeakers boom out the news on the same day a new queen is crowned. Crowds cheer madly —Everest has been conquered! Young Queen Elizabeth sends a telegram of congratulations.

In Katmandu, the king of Nepal rolls out a red carpet for the climbers. Thousands of people line the streets, and there's a parade three miles long. Tenzing is awarded the Star of Nepal. It is the highest honor of his native country.

Hillary and Tenzing fly to India, where Tenzing has lived for years. Twenty thou-

sand people mob them at the airport. India
issues postage stamps that bear both their

portraits. Some people even want to change Everest's name to Mount Tenzing.

Later, Queen Elizabeth bestows a great honor on Hillary. She makes him a knight—from now on he will be called *Sir* Edmund Hillary. Tenzing receives an important award called the George Medal from the queen. Streets in Britain are named after both heroes.

But some people begin to argue about the expedition. Which climber is better? Which man reached the summit first? Some believe Hillary is getting more credit than Tenzing since he is a white man and Tenzing is brown.

Hillary and Tenzing don't understand the fuss. Each knows he could not have succeeded without the other. And the two of them together wouldn't have stood a chance if it hadn't been for the teamwork of the whole expedition.

Tenzing becomes the head of a school that trains mountain climbers. Hillary explores the Antarctic and climbs more mountains. He even forms an expedition to hunt for the yeti.

Hillary also devotes himself to helping Sherpas. They are a very poor people. He raises money to build schools, a hospital, an airstrip, and many bridges. He and Tenzing stay friends.

Neither man ever climbs Everest again. They both feel a second try at the summit couldn't be as exciting.

But as the years pass, other climbers reach the top. Some take the path blazed by Hillary and Tenzing. Some create new challenges by trying different routes. Lighter and more advanced equipment makes their success possible.

Others want to find the easiest way up the mountain. They use computers to plan the best route, or they fly partway up by

helicopter. To them, nothing is as important as standing on the top.

There are even a few daring people who climb all the way without extra oxygen. One man, Reinhold Messner, accomplishes something truly incredible. In 1980, he reaches Everest's summit without an oxygen tank and all alone.

The earth's highest mountain is still a perilous place. More than a hundred climbers have died trying to reach the top. As long as humans seek to challenge themselves, some will head straight to Everest. A few will reach the summit—and many more will not.

Yet no matter how many people climb it, we'll always remember that first success. Everest was the mountain that would never be conquered—until Tenzing and Hillary made it to the top.